JOURNEYING
IN PLACE

Also by Gunilla Norris

BEING HOME

A Book of Meditations

BECOMING BREAD

Meditations on Loving and Transformation

SHARING SILENCE

Meditation Practice and Mindful Living

JOURNEYING IN PLACE

Reflections
from a
Country Garden

GUNILLA NORRIS

Drawings by Susan Mangam

BELL TOWER / NEW YORK

Copyright © 1994 by Gunilla Norris
Drawings copyright © 1994 by Crown Publishers, Inc.

Published by Bell Tower, an imprint of Harmony Books, a division of
Crown Publishers, Inc., 201 East 50th Street, New York, New York 10022.
Member of the Crown Publishing Group.

Random House, Inc. New York, Toronto, London, Sydney, Auckland

Bell Tower and colophon are trademarks of Crown Publishers, Inc.

Manufactured in the United States of America

Design by Jennifer Harper

Library of Congress Cataloging-in-Publication Data

Norris, Gunilla Brodde, 1939–
Journeying in place : reflections from a country garden / by
Gunilla Norris. — 1st ed.
p. cm.
1. Gardens—Religious aspects—Meditations.   2. Seasons—Religious
aspects—Meditations.   3. Norris, Gunilla Brodde, 1939–   . I. Title.
BL624.2.N67   1994
291.4′3—dc20   93-51088   CIP

ISBN 0-517-59762-4
10   9   8   7   6   5   4   3   2   1

First Edition

Mother was a constant beholder and appreciator of color and form. She could often be seen in small raptures at scenes and figures that impressed her. As a painter and tapestry designer she had individual exhibits in Portugal, Sweden, the United States, and Venezuela, as well as participating in many group shows. She was the winner of the Prix d'une Artiste Etrangère, the Salon des Femmes Peintres, and the Grand Prix International Clermont-Ferrand. Even on the very last day of her life, I saw her sketching on the inside of a book of matches.

She married my father, Gunnar Daniel Dryselius, in 1935 and served with him in the Swedish diplomatic corps until he retired as ambassador to Portugal. Their tours of duty took them to Czechoslovakia, Poland, Argentina, the United States, Venezuela, and ultimately Portugal.

She had three children: my sister, Anita; myself, Gunilla; and my brother, Jan. She was the grandmother of Bradford, Emily, Faith, Hillary, Jennifer, John, and Susanna.

A splendid-looking woman with much energy, she lived a full, dynamic life. Anna Christina was loved and is sorely missed. This book honors her.

Contents

All Saints' Day

I found my mother dead in the early morning on this day a year ago. All Saints' Day. In the Christian church calendar it is the day when the departed are celebrated and remembered. In the old Celtic and Anglo-Saxon calendars it is the day when the new year begins, first of November. The killing frost has happened both in my garden and in my life. I have lost my mother. The harvest has been gathered. The light has changed. The new year is at hand.

My farming ancestors took this season as an opportunity to begin again. When the fields were harvested and the soil turned, when the ground was frozen and the trees had lost their leaves, they were freed from their usual labors. Time could be spent in other ways, in storytelling, in fellowship, in preparing and repairing, in planning and reflecting, in remembering. I follow in their footsteps.

I want to go into memory now, to harvest my experiences and to share them. I want to make a journey through the landscape where I live, a journey *in place,* a journey through nature's year. Journey is really too active a word, for it implies a distance traveled from here to there. I do not mean that. I mean instead a circling in time, remembering a year as if it were all years. It is a way for me to honor my mother, experiencing the living of each season in celebration of her who gave me life.

For me recalling the seasons and the small particulars of my life is something like developing photographs. I have lived with a certain perspective, in very specific moments of time. They are my inner snapshots. Whether I am aware of it or not, the film has been exposed and developed. It holds my memory. Now the prints lie in the pan of developing fluid. What they really are is not yet known to me. But slowly, as they rise, I can see shapes take form. There is light and there is dark. I begin to see outlines, and when the prints finally float to the surface I see images reflecting my life back to me, ready for the light of day.

I have been deeply shaped by living in this small Connecticut landscape with its stone walls, its brook, its hemlocks and maples, its small wild creatures. I want to know what has happened to me here in this garden place, what entered my being while I conducted my so-called ordinary life of eating, sleeping, earning a living, and paying my taxes. I want to experience my prints developing so that the images become clear to me, so that I know what has touched and formed me.

The farmhouse I live in sits on a little more than two acres. Once the farm itself was big. It had pastures, woodlots, hay fields, orchards, and gardens. Now a lawn and a stand of ash trees grow where the apple orchard once flourished. I know where it was because the gnarled dead trunks remain as evidence. At the back of the property there is a little pond. No doubt it was a drinking place for cattle. In the town records this is simply another suburban house lot, with a given number, on a given street.

But I have come to know that in these two acres there is intense and quiet activity that is *happening* twenty-four hours a day. I miss most of it. I get caught up in what must be done and therefore fail to experience the sunsets, the budding of the raspberries, the rusting of old farm implements in the earth, the building of wasp nests, and the death of old trees. But I feel the vibration of it all and I want to know this eventfulness better. Even just a little bit better!

To know in this way requires my presence and an openness to experience. I have to be willing to be intimate, to surrender my goal-setting, direction-oriented, controlling, self-defining self, in order to be encountered, to be met, to have a chance to be known. This is hard for me. The urge to be in control is so embedded in my body, my education, my culture, I feel helpless under its illusion.

That control and intimacy are mutually exclusive I know. Intimacy cannot be commanded or planned. It is not willed but happens by grace and opens the inner doors of the heart. It more readily happens when I lay no claim to anything and discover instead what is already present, already given.

All true intimacies are gifts. They appear as if from behind us, beside us, above us, below us. We usually cannot see them coming. They take our whole attention, and in the process we have a chance to come face-to-face with something we did not know about ourselves and the world.

To commune, to discover and to be discovered is deeply human. Real convergences are revelations that lift us out of ourselves, out of recoiling from any aspect of reality. We experience the Self then—all possessive pronouns gone—the joy of existence, which is the light within everything, the light that burns for its own sake declaring, "I am that I am." In that light, death, too, is experienced as a central part of life.

The Latin word for intimate is *intimus,* "inmost." I know that when I live in an "inmost" manner here in this old farm lot I see and know much more about the world and myself. I come to experience that each thing that dwells here with me is a saint of sorts. These are the presences, the events and experiences —the "inner photos"—I want to develop. To re-member, to hold, and to venerate the life around me, which sustains me, is a way to honor my personal mother. It is also a way to celebrate our common mother, the earth—the first and primary intimacy from which all other intimacy develops.

I hope as you read that you will think of the saints of the place where you live, whether that be a city street or a forest. The saints are all equal. They ask us to participate, to be fully here on earth. The fulcrum of this universe may ultimately be a passionate mutuality in which we surrender any separate definition of ourselves and discover that we are who we are together—in fundamental communion—in relationship with everything that is.

Newtown, Connecticut

November 1992

FALL

Leaves

---

*T*here are so many of them. Piles of them. I take pleasure in their abundance. More saints than you could ever dream of. Each one singular. Each one itself. Yellow, red, orange, parchment. They sail down in the autumn air like fearless sky divers. They are so trusting—letting go completely. Not questioning as I do . . . Will it be safe? Will I understand? Will it hurt? . . . stalling, qualifying, questioning, instead of releasing and taking to the air.

In the order of things here on my road the ash trees shed first. Their boatlike leaves sail away undramatically and early. After that the big sugar maple begins. It stands in perfect glory for about a week.

Then one windless night I sense that it sighs deeply somewhere inside its gnarled trunk and says, "Enough." The next day I see a waterfall of leaves. They fall, no, cascade down, rustling, pouring, to pool upon the ground like a large, golden puddle. Yellow earth-light illumines my face.

I have felt that glow before. On her last night my mother was aglow like that. She was radiant. Neither of us knew it was her last night. Standing in the kitchen she blazed like the maple tree and I said to her, "Mother, you are so beautiful." She smiled and nodded. "I have the glory in me," she said. Then quietly during the night, something in her declared, "Enough," and she shed her body. She let go. It was utterly clean. Only light remained.

Messy as the autumn leaves are in the yard, their process is clean. When the time comes to let go, they let go. With the help of my friend Keith, I take up the rake and we get the leaves to the compost pile. Heaps and heaps of leaves.

In grieving also, the affairs of the deceased must be gathered and gone through. The body is buried, and the composting of memory begins—the mystery of the years, layers and layers of shared life turning to soil in one's being.

I can feel it in myself. It is like a slow and constant heat. In this process I am aware that I cannot know what is happening until months later, sometimes years later. As in the decomposition of leaves, the *matter* of it all begins to alter. Memory shifts without my knowing about it. The very substance changes. Insights emerge. My own aging, like the weather, adds its part to this as does the living of every moment. As the heat continues the old breaks down and I experience something new emerging.

In my compost pile on the hill the leaves are of all different kinds. There are grass clippings too, weeds, small twigs, and kitchen leavings. As I turn the pile over everything joins with everything else. It is hard to know any longer what is what because it is mixed together, on the way to becoming one thing, soil. I take comfort in this. Through the seasons my memories are composted, too, and like the leaves they come together. Turned over and over, in time they finally turn into something new—rich, dark earth in the palm of my hand.

The Feral Cat

I have seen him now for seven years. These are only glimpses—maybe two or three in the course of many months. I sense him more than I see him . . . a somewhat savage shadow that moves. His fur is the color of underbrush, thick and matted. He could be mistaken for a raccoon except when he turns his face toward me and looks. Then I can see that he is a feral cat, and very fine. I like knowing that he hunts and survives on this property.

Him is how I think of the cat. All my instincts tell me he should have no name, for his power lies in the fact that he is wild and is determined to be so. I think of him as a homeless one and I would wish him whatever comfort there can be. Of course, as I think this, he lies under the lattices of the porch next to the warm foundation behind which the furnace churns and chugs.

If I happen to cross his path in the morning he hurries under the boxwood with a haughty turn of his head. I feel as if I have stepped on his private domain. And, of course, I have. He moved in here before I did.

My best look at him came one sunny day in mid-November. He had found a bank of leaves where sun would continue to shine for many hours. Snuggled down in brown brush and russet leaves, he disappeared except for the tufts of his ears. He knew I had seen him, and there was a challenge in his eyes. A feral saint. I couldn't take my eyes off him and he knew it.

We sat this way, he in the leaves and I in my chair, with the windowpane between us. The sun beat down. The minutes passed and then the hour. I felt akin to him and could feel myself becoming catlike there in the leaves.

I could smell the wet, cold ground somehow, and the slightly dusty odor of leaves. I could feel warmth coming into me, reaching past fur to the bones, white precise bones. I could hear the rustle of a starling. Not worth hunting. Not worth moving my thawing body for. I could feel the rightness of this

7

bank, this place where no one owed me anything and I was free to be myself, free to care for myself. Hunt when hungry. Rest when tired.

I knew all the places to go. Under the lattice, into the leaf pile, close to the brush heaps in the woods to wait for grouse or chipmunk. I knew where the water was. I knew where to be when. This is not any kind of special time telling. Noon and sun are the same thing. Shade and hiding, one. Lunch and rabbit, a perfect unity. Something in me knew when to move and when to be still . . . my own nature . . . taking in the warmth, being here, homelessly at home.

I could see myself through the cat's eyes. I could sense his thinking, . . . "That one behind the glass . . . she's such a pale thing . . . no wildness in her. Safe and limited. Groomed. Careful. Predictable. Let her look. Let her see the other choice. Let her remember her own fur."

No address. No name. Ugly. Wild. Sensible. Living with no trace. Feral . . . free!

Mice

---

*B*y Thanksgiving the herb and vegetable gardens are all cleaned up. Dry stalks of tomato plants and twiggy stems of rosemary have been pulled from the ground. The yellow snarl of frozen nasturtium and the upright, black spotted remains of basil have been removed. Now I can see the small holes of animals in the ground, underground passageways and winter mansions of chipmunks and mice. Unbeknownst to me there has been careful construction under the canopy of late summer leaves.

Convenient food supplies are tucked away, and strategic entries made into the old cellar of the farmhouse. I know, because at this time of year I hear cautious scurrying at night. The mice are taking up their winter life.

There is no way to keep them out of this house and garden. I have to share the place. The truth is that we live side by side, an intimate arrangement. There is only one of me, and many of them.

One year all my grass seed was consumed. I had carefully put it in a metal container in the garage, but by spring it was nothing but chaff. So, too, the birdseed. The first year I lived with this, I felt frantic. Was my place infested? Were the mice chewing the electrical wires? Would I have to keep everything in metal tins? I put out traps. By the time the new growing season came there were still mice in the cellar. I considered poison. What to do?

I did not want to go on a killing rampage. I did not want to let the situation get out of hand. I never solved this quandary, but my attitude changed. It happened in the spring when I inadvertently found a mouse nest on a shelf in the garage. The nest was in, and also made of, an old mattress cover I used as a painting dropcloth. Curled up, surrounded by shredded fabric and cotton batting, were six baby mice . . . blind, hairless, and oh so vulnerable. I could see their hearts beating right through the skin. Their little chests heaved with each breath. They were a pink pulsing so sheer it could be snuffed out in an instant.

They must have been born only hours before. Could they sense their danger? Was the mother watching? Questions rose in me as fast as my awe at the vulnerability of these newborns. To be born is to be utterly exposed. I remember the sheer newness of my own two children when they were first born.

Then it struck me that each time I come into newness I, too, am pink like this, pulsing, and vulnerable. It has happened many times in my life, not just on day one. New relationships, new dwellings, new jobs, new understandings. My eyes do not quite function. My skin is paper thin. It is always a sheer time, an intimate time, when, like all newborns, I need protection badly.

So, of course, I left the nest just where it was, and some of my intolerant attitude also. Two weeks later the baby mice were gone. They were functioning. They were in the field, being field mice, not house mice. I shook out the dropcloth and thought about the *able* part of the word *vulnerable*. Able to sustain injury is what vulnerable means. Right!

Mice, who seem so skittery and afraid, are actually a brave lot. They have given me a new definition of brave—to feel the fear one has and to own it. Those who deny their fear are not brave.

By now I have looked a few mice directly in the eye. Encountered this way, they bristle out their whiskers like antennae. Their tiny black button eyes are unquestioning and steady. My admiration has grown with each of these exchanges.

The mice come and go. I come and go. When I am having Thanksgiving turkey, they are having seeds. So far they have not taken over the house. They are actually a modest few, for the local cat and the big black snake keep the population under control. Now when I hear rustling under the sink I am more willing to share . . . I have to, in any case. It is the nibbling saints, in autumn mode, sharing my house. And I *do* give thanks.

Bulldog

---

*S*trictly speaking Putnam does not reside in my
garden. He lives catty-corner down the road.
Still and all, I feel Putnam lives here, too, for he is in
my yard often enough. His body, only six inches off
the ground, wags its way into the driveway. His coat
is an auburn, almost red color and ripples around
him. Putnam is a very fat English bulldog of some
advanced years.

His face looks as if he had pressed it up against
the shop window of a dog delicatessen for weeks on
end. I think his customary drool comes from gazing at
those juicy bones displayed in a charcuterie for bull-
dogs just like him. He lifts his face toward me with

the innocence of a child and waits for me to love him.

Of course, I stop everything and give Putnam the attention his unselfconscious and enthusiastic presence seems to require. There is something natural, nonchalant, and humorous about his behavior. I smile and pet Putnam, and feel something else as well, something uncomfortable. When I look deeper into this discomfort I know I am embarrassed by Putnam.

His delight is obvious and flagrant. He turns over and presents his roly-poly stomach for stroking. "Put your hand right there. Good! A little higher, please." Wiggle, wiggle, the sausage body moves along the loose stones of the driveway positioning itself to get the perfect sensation. There seems to be no pride in the dog, just direct, unadulterated pleasure seeking . . . hence the name my daughter-in-law and I have given him privately . . . Putnam, the Pleasure Pig.

I wonder how different life would be for me if I could be as lacking in self-doubt and self-judgment as Putnam. His whole being demonstrates an assumption that he is a lovable creature, a deserving creature, and an enjoyable one. His fat, aged self simply squirms with the sacred knowledge that he is one of God's creatures. Such direct light makes me turn my eyes away.

To act as if one had the total endorsement of the

universe behind one's particular existence would be extraordinary! I hedge my bets by offering to others what I myself want, by restricting my requests for love and help to those I know will not reject me out of hand. I am oh, so careful, whereas I could, with a Putnam-like trust, meet the world with a joyful, natural wag.

I study Putnam and try to unlearn my embarrassment. Someone told me once that embarrassment was misplaced radiance. What is rightly placed radiance? It must have something to do with the glowing ease of being what one is, and feeling the endorsement of belonging to life itself.

I observe Putnam's ease. He lies in the middle of the road where the sun shines and warms the tarmac. If he must, he moves for cars. Mostly cars move for him. And if it should happen that his desirous, loving nature does not meet with appropriate affection, he walks off with a "too-bad-for-them" attitude. Not daunted or belittled in the slightest, he seeks his own counsel and pleasure under the mailbox. Neither will Putnam reject because he was rejected. He will be open to pleasure again . . . meeting a stranger or an old acquaintance with renewed interest in the possibilities of exchange. No smoldering grudges here or careful tallies of past slights.

Putnam is not, in fact, trying to attain something. He is simply meeting the world with his pleasure-nature, inviting those who can to join his radiance . . . light with light. I want to participate in this direct and happy warmth. I want to let my love and pleasure out so it can meet the love and pleasure of others directly.

WINTER

White Ash

It's late December. The leaves have all fallen and the trees stand naked. Stripped, the trees have a sculptured look, and I have the curious sensation that I can both see and hear better in these winter woods. The wind is blowing hard. Above my head, tree limbs are clashing, making boisterous, wooden music. Here below, where I stand, the trunks seem to glow. On their bark the lichen shimmers in the blue-gray light of this season. Subtle, muted colors . . . ochre, gray-white and the palest moss green . . . patinas made by slow quiet growth.

This is the stuff of life and of art. Nothing dramatic . . . just years of persistence . . . growing in the same place . . . extending a little farther . . . becoming a little more. A quiet work that enlarges by seasons. I think of my mother, whose art grew quietly, persistently throughout her whole life.

What is homely and seemingly inconsequential becomes important in winter. In this woodlot of stripped ash trees and brush, one little bush shines with red berries. The berries seem to shout with color. "We are here," they call to the birds. "Eat us, digest us, spread our seeds so we can multiply." This is interrelatedness with a purpose.

But the berries do something else as well with no obvious purpose. Their color, in this otherwise brown and green canvas, makes it possible to see everything more clearly. Twenty red berries in an acre of brown. The stripped trees make the berries visible. The berries make the ash trees visible. They reveal and reflect one another and yet remain independent. Together they are more without losing themselves. In winter light this is so visible to me. It is pure interplay. I want my human relationships to have this intimacy, this ease.

Bare bones of ash trees . . . shimmering berries . . . lichen growing without ambition, just true to its lichen nature. When I allow myself to be and allow others to be just as they are, what wonderful bare bones of connection that is. When I can notice and savor the many flashes of color that happen in life, the bright berries of delight, what constant praise that is. When I can be patient and know that what develops over time . . . little by little . . . with consistency . . . is what ultimately is rewarded and lasts, what wonderful relaxation in growth that is. I can stop hurrying to be what I cannot yet be, and rest simply in what I am now.

Above me the leafless crowns of the ash trees move against each other. The sound is that of wooden tongues speaking or singing a foreign language with glottal stops. I do not understand a word, but I feel the music. Something happens in my belly when I hear it. Somehow I am singing, too, and being sung . . . it is a different kind of understanding. Fifteen feet above my head a grand, important orchestra is playing the winter chorale of the white ashes.

Wooden voices singing a capella in the chill wind. I listen and feel the wordless branches in myself, joining the allegro. It is winter solstice time. The dark turns again to light. I feel called to praise. Oh, sing the turning of the year. Sing the season. Sing with whatever can sing. Clap hands and branches. Let all that has life be glad. More understanding than my life can wish for is this urge to praise. Rejoice and again rejoice!

Tracks on New Snow

*D*ecember thirty-first. The new calendar year will start tomorrow. I am aware that it is a year my mother will not share. My breath catches and I go outside.

New snow has fallen. That helps. Like a white sheet of beautiful paper, the snow is a parchment ready for writing. I will read many things on this paper. It will inform me.

My friend Jack, a longtime observer of nature, says that he can feel the presence and mystery of a creature almost more strongly in its tracks than in its appearance. One can study life-as-lived in animal tracks, life-as-process, the marks of what has been and still is, somehow simultaneously together.

One can dream oneself into those blue-black shadows in the snow and sense the motivation of another creature. I am sure that in the white snow cover of our minds our intentions are marking dark tracks all the time. I know there are beaten paths, entrenched habits, that keep me from exploring new ground. I am not aware of those trails and how deeply they have been laid down in me. I do not even know the self who treads upon them.

To study motivation is to study one's own tracks. Is there time to catch that movement which is before movement? The movement, like an animal's instinct, prior to thought, and alive in the very cells themselves? That movement which forms thought, which is the substance and event of thought? This is where those old predators, fear and desire, can be faced. This is the place where true self-expression will be discovered, if it ever can be.

In the fine white snow of this December day I see how a rabbit came this way into brushy piles by the stone wall. Was it escaping . . . running in fear? Was it foraging . . . trying to feed the constant desire of its stomach? Was it leaping for the sheer joy of movement? Rabbit tracks . . . I dream myself into the vulnerable creature that made them . . . so much like me. Heart pounding a mile a minute, often stopped and frozen in fear, or scurrying for cover.

This white snow is like an empty mind. It is beautiful. Without tracks it is beautiful. With tracks it is beautiful. I can learn here. I can discover experiences occurring, moment by moment, like small explosions . . . the "big bangs," albeit in miniature, of this constantly becoming world.

I follow the rabbit's path. The back paws leave bigger shadows. There is something even, rhythmic, in the spaces between front paws and back, in the repeating of their pattern. I follow, and leave my own pattern in the new snow.

One time last winter I saw some tracks stop: Hip hop . . . hip hop . . . hip hop . . . and then complete stop. Unbroken snow. No evidence of violence. No explanation. No continuation. No tracks anywhere. Nothing but white snow.

Was the rabbit transmuted? A transfigured saint? An "Assumption"? I don't know. It is a mystery. I smile to feel again how life-giving the unsolvable is. I want to live with mystery . . . bounding into the heart of the world, into the new snow of this moment and the new year.

Thaw

---

*F*ebruary. The days are getting lighter. I feel relief. The sun, for the past two weeks or more, is
warmer. I can hear the water running in the brook,
which was dry only a few weeks back. Everything is
trickling. Little rivulets of water move in the grass,
among tree roots, under the leaves. Walking out in
the woods I find that my shoes stick in the soft
ground. As I raise my boot, the earth makes a ṣlurpy,
muddy sound, as of juicy, exaggerated kissing.

Sm-a-a-a-ck! This sound makes me smile. The
soles of my feet are happy. I am enjoying this. It's February and close to Valentine's Day. I am celebrating wet
earth. I am celebrating a break in the below-twenty

degrees that has been so relentless for the past weeks. February thaw . . . messy and wonderful. I can almost sniff spring, though it is not an odor that can actually be smelled.

This is the time to see what winter damage has happened in the garden. It is the time to pore over seed catalogs, and to keep my gardener's greed in check. Living alone, I know I am limited in what I can do . . . just so much! I have to be willing to look at the glossy catalogs and say, "NO."

In this mild winter weather everything appears hopeful and possible. A little more sun and the garden looks as if it is already blooming—weed-free and glorious. This is an image I have learned not to trust, for by late June, with too much to take care of, the pleasure of this garden turns into a chore. Then I grumble. I resent everything to do with maintenance. I have no leisure and hence no delight.

Leisure and delight . . . they are wedded. Without leisure there is no time to feel and to savor. Their rhythm allows things to grow at an organic pace. If I can really match that pace I will recall that the "inmost" garden of the world is fundamentally leisurely. Vegetation has its seasons. The moon has its month. The sun has its day. The universe is orderly and is always on time.

I look at the seed catalogs and from them I get an artificial sense that anything and everything can be grown. With effort and at a price! If I forced flowers, started seeds, bought artificial light, I could have something splendid even now in the winter gloom. But this I have painfully learned is not for me. Having lost my leisure over and over again, I must be abstinent now in order to have what I really need . . . time to feel and to be in the place I live. It's February and that means it is winter still, a time when I can be spare and love it.

Spare . . . knowing that less is more. Less need to improve, less trying, less judgment, less regret. I am learning about this, year after year. Slowly the self-imposed abstinence gives me freedom. This is not always an easy process. It often feels like dying. Perhaps I am practicing for the day when I will have to give up everything, when I will be in another garden altogether.

To say "no" to hurry, to overwork, to whatever is more than is needed, is to say "yes" to leisure, to reverie, to communion. It is a "dying-to-live" process. I want this to be my February thaw.

Out into this mild, winter weather I go to reconnoiter and to pick up small sticks for kindling. I cannot do anything about the garden now. This is the season when the garden is truly and simply lying fallow. And I must follow suit. In that state, restoration goes on in ways that are not apparent and are yet essential. For me that means going out into the world of snow puddles and melting icicles instead of ordering seeds. It means experiencing the land without a plan for it.

As I walk in the woodlot my shoes make a squashy sound. Suddenly something moves near the brush piles. A loud bounding. Then I see the white flag of a deer make a few graceful arcs up over the nearby ridge and out of sight. My heart pounds a little with the surprise.

I notice now that I am suddenly alert, that I have exchanged any notion of efficiency for the experience of attentiveness. With the movement of another creature I have remembered my creatureliness. I feel a confirmation in this. I am in ever present time now, God's time, alive time.

I can feel the melting world—everything wet and waiting. The leaves, matted down since they first fell, can be picked up in sheets, almost like filo dough. Deep down the ground is still frozen. February . . . full of spring, and full of cold that is yet to come.

I listen to the brook water running in the culvert and down into my neighbor's yard. It moves along at a happy, burbling pace, flowing with a steady volume. It stays within its banks. It follows the path of least resistance and is yet consistent with itself. Trickling, gurgling, bubbling . . . on it goes . . . not missing any ground it travels over . . . filling up the hollow spaces . . . moving on . . . moving on. I want to garden and to live this way. Staying within my capacity. Filling the space. Enjoying each season. Planting, cultivating, pruning, harvesting, lying fallow. Moving on in God's time, leisure time . . . thawing into spring.

Geese

___

 *S*ome distance to the east and north of me are two large airports. When I am outside I can hear the droning of the planes in their flying pattern over this section of the county. The silver bodies glint above the tips of the ash trees. Their white contrails leave patterns in the sky. These 747s have been places, and in the brief moment they fly above this small suburban plot I feel a sympathetic nudge from the faraway. Every year I have flown to Europe to see my mother. No need this year. Everything seems to remind me of that. No need. Not this year.

Geese come flying over, too. They land at their own local airports . . . two large bodies of water to the southeast and west of me. Much of the water supply for the county is drawn from these reservoirs. Most of the geese winter here, but some have been to other continents, filling their feathers with heat and tropical air. It's early March and they have returned. I like knowing where they have been, especially in this cold snap.

Sometimes there are only a few birds flying in formation. Sometimes there are twenty or more. I get a rush of hopeful feeling when I hear them honking. I have never completely understood why. At first I thought it was because they had the freedom of the skyways . . . something high and romantic . . . something in contrast to my earthbound existence. But lately I have learned more about geese through an article a friend brought to share. This new information has fleshed out that spontaneous inner feeling of mine.

What I learned is that of all the creatures that I can see in this landscape, the geese best represent the communion of saints. They depend on one another. The lead goose does the most work, but when it is tired, it falls back and another takes its place. To be able to rely on others is a deep trust that does not come easily.

The geese fly in the wake of one another's wings. They literally get a lift from one another. I want to be with others this way. Geese tell me that it is, indeed, possible to fly with equals.

The high honking I hear when I stand on the ground and look up is the sound of encouragement the geese make to keep on flying. It is a loud and happy sound in my ears. I want to honk with others on the journey.

The geese fly over, signaling what it is to be in communion and community. My heart feels glad. The old victory sign was a V. The geese make this sign as they fly by. And I do the same with my fingers raised high in snappy salute.

SPRING

Peepers

I listen for them now. They are to me the first sound of spring. In the early mornings their high trill begins to rise from the cattle pond and the nearby marsh. A life sign.

I have never laid eyes on them. But as spring advances their chorus grows until there is a continuous high pitch day and night. "The waters are warm enough. The sun is warm enough. Live," they sing. "Come forward. Live."

In old Scandinavian lore fires are burned on the last day of April. These fires are meant to melt Old Man Winter down to the ground. Young folk jump over the embers. Couples make love.

People drink and dance and embrace the new season.

Just before May Day last year my siblings and I took our mother's ashes and buried them. Rain fell in sheets that April day. It was bleak. Although yellow tulips could be bought in the florist shops there was a bitter chill in the air. We were frozen to the core. The awesomeness of placing the urn with our mother's remains down in the stony vault next to our father's urn was bone sobering. These were only the ashes. Not our parents. We said this to one another and gazed further back into the vault where the urns of those before them stood solemnly. Grandmother. Grandfather.

We said the words of passage, and tried to sing in our wavering voices the hymns we had picked. We sounded very feeble and off-key in the rain, in the cold, in the bleak truth that our parents were gone. I think we buried a little of ourselves there. And we took with us the certain knowledge that we are the generation now living, the one on which our children lean.

As we rode back from the cemetery the minibus was full of silence. Only the monotonous flip-flop of the windshield wipers counted off the kilometers. From time to time, between cloudbursts, we had glimpses of the countryside. There we could see the fields dotted with big brush piles. Prunings, windfall, and building scraps, gathered for almost a year, lay ready for the torch on Walpurgis Night, the night when the cold is burned to the ground.

These rituals help. Smelling the smoke the night following the burial we could cry a little more easily. I know now that I am mourning my mother through every season of the year. We all mourn this way. The first Christmas without the beloved, the first New Year. We will feel the loved one not here for the first bloom of forsythia, not here for the ripening of the pears, not here . . . not here. . . .

The peepers are wailing. How is it that one feels loss so much more deeply in spring than at any other time? Loss moves like a drill through my body, like the high-pitched voices of these young frogs. But they are singing a new song. "The sun is warm enough. The waters are warm enough. Live. Come on. Live!"

Saints Shrill. Hundreds of them. Could it be that by sheer dint of their noisy insistence the last of Old Man Winter melts into water and runs off, taking a portion of grief along in the bargain?

Skunk Cabbage

S kunk cabbages begin to poke their leaves out of the mud. In the low-lying parts of the woodlot their hefty leaves push and prod forward into spring. They are the free-form sculptures of these woods. You either like them or hate them. They grow in profusion. I had better like them, it seems.

It is early April now. The mosquitoes have laid their larvae on the stagnant water between the dark green leaves of the skunk cabbages. Birds call. Buds are knobbing up on the trees and bushes. I feel an ache in the air . . . the swollen ache of life pushing forward, bursting its seams.

Determined to watch the cabbages grow, I have

been going out to inspect their progression. The upward surge of the leaves is astounding. You can almost hear them growing, sopping up moisture. They gain an inch a day, it seems. This is cabbage intelligence. They must do this while it's wet enough. They must do this while the canopy of the trees is not shutting the light out for their initial growth.

I think how something in me wants to grow, too, when the opportunity is at hand. There is an urgency . . . an "it-won't-wait" feeling. But to really experience this, and to act on it, is not so easy. It means listening.

I practice with the cabbages. I listen to them. Are they humming? Buzzing? I sense a vibration without sound that is yet a sound. I hear/feel it. Can I learn to hear/feel the same in me? I think this is the sound the Bible speaks of . . . "In the beginning was the Word." In the beginning was the Word, meaning the Vibration, I believe. All that exists has been sounded. I think we are configured through this noiseless vibration which is movement and being all at once. We are named by it, oscillated, electromagnetically uttered into life.

To listen, then, to the name we are given to be, is a profound act of resonance. I think Saint Cabbage does it sitting there . . . squat and green . . . firmly planted in the sump of the woods. It obeys its given nature. I want to be as secure in mine, to feel the vibration that is naming me from the soles of my feet to the roots of my hair. And since a part of that naming is to bear my drawbacks, I ask to learn to stink as the cabbages do, directly. No psychic deodorant. No cover-up. I want to believe that these stocky, green skunks of the woods are giving me, their two-legged friend, a hearty encouragement from deep within the muck and ooze of spring and the vernal equinox.

Wildflowers

---

*T*he leaves are out. They are a sheer light green, and I am surprised by their shadows. Now I see patterns on the ground again, patches of dark and light. My feet walk a dappled path.

A sweet smell wafts toward the house from the woods. When I first smelled it, I thought a very special plant must be the source. It took a while to determine that this scent was Essence of Eastern Woods, a combination of organic matter, young ferns, and wildflowers. Over the years I have waited for that odor. A quiet smell that is utterly intimate. It opens me.

This is the time to hunt for Dutchman's

breeches, patches of green with a hovering cloud of white pantaloonlike flowers. Now is the time to find the light pink of wild geranium, and the deep magenta of trilliums hidden under their trefoil leaves. Solomon's seal is out. The ferns are uncurling. Jack is preaching in his pulpit. Indian pipe and lady's slipper, those protected species, are also emerging. They are all there in their appointed places, shy woodland saints. I love finding them again and again, predictable and wild, elusive and perennial. The woods fill with their sweetness.

In spiritual texts there is mention of perfumed states of mind. In deep concentration odors can be perceived so honeylike that one is called to remember the beauty of the soul. Maybe that is why we are drawn to very specific fragrances, fragrances that remind us of our deepest being. And is not smell the most intimate of the senses? We inhale odor, we take it deeply into us.

The wildflower saints provoke me to remember the steadiness of return, year after year. They tell me that one does not need to be cultivated to be beautiful. They tell me that the soul remembers its essence, if it is given room to grow. I bow to the shy trillium, the wild geranium, the jack-in-the-pulpit, the lady's slipper, the Dutchman's breeches, the Indian pipes, the ferns, Solomon's seal, and the columbine.

These gentle flowers remind me that we surrender to no one finally but to our own soul, to the essence of ourselves, which is hidden in God. Sweet and wild is the experience of surrender. There is nothing more intimate.

Purple Finches

A pair of purple finches begins to circle the house in late April. This is their territory. They look for a likely spot and begin gathering twigs, bits of string, pine needles, and other nest-building materials. He is rosy and large. She is mostly gray, and smaller.

The two are now old friends of mine. I like to guess where they'll put their nests this time. They build two . . . a false one as a decoy and the real one. Mrs. Finch even sits in the decoy nest to fool the predatory world.

One year the real nest was built in the decorative wreath on the front door. I could not believe my good fortune in being able to watch their nesting ingenuity from indoors. Unfortunately someone else was watching, too. Four eggs of a lovely blue-green color were laid. When the eggs were almost ready to hatch the nest was raided by the neighbor's black cat. I was heartbroken.

The finches came back the following year and built a nest on the porch light fixture . . . a little higher than the cat could reach. But from then on I knew that their real nest was hidden high in the hemlock while the decoys were easy to see somewhere on available ledges around the house.

I have noticed this decoy maneuver in myself also. I will often look very busy about something entirely different to keep safe the brooding and hatching of something precious. I build a decoy activity, so to speak, for I know that too much light, or outside interest, directed toward a creative inner process pillages the nest. Nothing can hatch.

To incubate a book, a poem, a drawing, an idea, or a new attitude, I need an inner nest. The twigs of association must be gathered. The materials to make a safe place for incubation must be quietly put together. If this process is disturbed a whole new nest must be built. I have to start over. But I cannot start over too many times. There is not enough psychic strength.

For myself the secret of secrecy is to tell *all* to

someone I love and trust, if the secret is about pain or shame of any kind. But if the secret is about an inner process that needs time to develop, then I must wait until the pregnancy is far enough along to bear exposure.

Turtles cover their eggs. Finches build decoy nests. Mothers grow silently large with child. We have an instinct to surround the new with time, with protection, with secrecy. I am grateful for the ways this has been done for me.

I have yet to see any baby finches. My purple pair do a good job of protecting their brood. I feel good about their skill in this. New creatures are born for their own sake, for their own lives, not for the benefit of parents or curious bystanders. Like books, like paintings, like poems. . . .

I am simply grateful that Mr. and Mrs. Finch find this garden good enough to raise a family in. May the little saints fly in their own time.

Dahlias

I go down into the cellar and find dahlia tubers from the fall. They are wizened ugly things. I can hardly believe these brown and wrinkled lumps of matter are going to be flowers in less than two months.

It is early May now and the ground is warming up. Even if we should have one more frost these tubers will be safe in the ground. I have tried to sort out their colors so that I will have mostly white and yellow flowers. Right now the tubers all look the same and I have a kind of color roulette on my hands. By the end of June there may be a bank of yellow and white dahlias punctuated by a solitary, flaming red one. A surprise. A red flag. So be it!

I feel glad to be in my shirtsleeves, trowel in hand. The west side of the house has a stone wall close to its foundation. A bed has been dug there, and that is where the dahlias are going.

These are the small variety and do not have to be set very deeply in the ground. I spade up the dirt and put one of the tubers in. By fall this one will have produced several more, not unlike potatoes. I just have to wait.

This is easy gardening. I like it, and yet I am a little suspicious about easy things. Pop the tuber in and forget it. If the weather is dry, add water. It's a foolproof recipe. I feel a little ashamed when I get compliments on any of my fast and easy recipes . . . it seems the results shouldn't be that good with so little effort.

This, of course, is Northern European conditioning. Hard is good. Easy is soft and suspicious. These private or cultural evaluations have nothing to do with how things fundamentally are. The intrinsic way must be the easiest way, and I want to learn to trust that now. Standing by the stone wall I ask myself: "What is doing the growing around here?" I answer: "Something in the dahlias themselves. I am simply present to enjoy this."

I spade up a place in the bank for each tuber. In

they go! I replace the earth. I do not have to do anything more. I do not have to sweat. The dahlias know what to do. Leaves will come. Flowers will come. Some years they will even be profuse. Then the dahlias will die. I will dig up the tubers. I will put them in the cellar. And they will be planted again the following year if all things remain the same. Which is as likely to be true as not to be true.

Can I live this dahlia way, too? A way that does not complicate, does not avoid, or force things to happen? A direct way that simply opens . . . allowing for process? To plant, to flower in the sun, and to surrender to frost when it comes, this way is thorough. It occurs in every aspect of life and skips nothing. It is living and dying, again and again. It is so simple, this allowing, and so profound. I read in the dictionary that the root meaning of the word *suffer* is *allow*. This stirs me.

In the pale May sunshine, with a tuber in each hand, I ask: What is easy? What is hard? I don't know. They are all mixed up now in my mind. But I do know that these tubers, wizened root balls, are full of summer color . . . full of allowing. Saint Dahlia. As I tuck you into soil, I want to trust that I am tucked in, too, embedded in that matrix which supports all form. Then whatever color is within me will emerge with little effort.

Poison Ivy

*M*ay. The poison ivy leaves are beginning to come out on the vines. They are slightly copper-colored and oily. Poison ivy grows happily in this county of Connecticut. In fact, it is the most luxuriant crop on this property. By June its leaves will be glossy and green. If they did not cause such a skin disturbance they would be a most popular ground cover.

I have learned to respect the plant and watch out for it. A cake of yellow soap is always at hand by the kitchen sink in case I inadvertently brush up against these leaves. Some people handle their poison with poison. They spray, year after year, and eventually some parts of their gardens are free of the vines. I do not feel comfortable with this method for I do not know what other effects I will be causing.

I do not feel comfortable doing nothing either. John, my son, put copper nails in the thick hairy vines growing up the trunks of maple and ash. Some of the vines he severed. But this has very little effect on their profusion.

I notice that wherever there is a great deal of poison ivy, there is also a bounty of jewelweed. They are companion plants. From jewelweed a very fine itching salve can be made. Things are often paired up like this in nature. They balance each other and form a whole of some sort.

This happens in the internal ecology, too. I see in myself how an extreme of any kind always constellates the opposite. If I fall into work addiction my body will sooner or later give out and I will have to experience doing absolutely nothing for a period of time. If I pride myself on being a thoughtful and consistently courteous person, I am sure to turn unexpectedly vicious.

The poison will form and will surely find its way to expression. An antidote is needed. I can see this balancing act very clearly in the consuming of foods. If I eat too much sugar I want something salty to go with it. If I use a heavy stimulant I want something bland to soothe my nervous system.

Poison ivy and jewelweed. Over time it is never just one or the other. How often have I thought I was absolutely right about something, and in being adamant I lost the fabric of relatedness and the situation became all wrong. I keep forgetting that events arise in relationship to each other. They grow simultaneously. They are neither this nor that . . . and yet they occur because of this and that. They make each other happen.

Something that looks like poison may lead to something very good. Something seemingly wonderful can have the seeds of destruction in it. I have no way of being sure . . . the living of that tension is so very hard. I will always be right and wrong. Safe and in danger. Strong and weak. Loving and uncaring. Stupid and smart. Aware and unconscious.

I know this as I walk here in the woodlot and despair over the profusion of green and glossy leaves. Too much to ever be rid of! These leaves are here for good, like the ivy inside me. I take comfort in the stately stands of jewelweed that grow here as well— tall, tumescent, with lovely little orange flowers. May they be inside me, too.

With the poison is the jewel, and vice versa. Ivy and weed. Two kinds of saints. They are my teachers. I hold them in mind, and a bar of yellow soap in hand.

The Quince Tree

I have wondered if my old quince tree dates back as far as the original structure of the farmhouse, 1840? The quince is in bloom now. Its little white flowers are such a contrast to its dark brown trunk. They shine and are completely new while the tree itself looks ancient. Twisted and gnarled, it appears to me like an aged, modern dancer, whose every limb is going off in some contorted, asymmetrical direction. Here and there bark has peeled off in long strips, to hang like a skimpy dance costume around the exposed trunk.

Every year I think that this will be the last year for the old tree. And then here it is again . . . in bloom. By late August its furry, pearlike fruit will be hanging there for the birds and for me. Some years there are only two or three quinces. Sometimes I gather as many as ten.

I respect this tree very much. It is the crone of the garden. And though it is, in fact, rather ugly, I would miss its presence very much should a winter wind take it down. Its dark shape in the middle of a very green lawn seems appropriate. A great-great-grandmother tree that is still bearing fruit.

I observe Mother's Day with this old tree. I cannot call my mother anymore. I miss that very much. I cannot call my grandmother. I am the grand-mother now and I do not know how to really be that. Not yet, anyway. So I stand here in the garden and try to feel the old tree.

I want to learn from it. One thing I have un-derstood is that I can bear fruit even into the later years of my life. I see that in the tree. It also tells me of the power of roots. This tree would not be stand-ing now without some wonderful taproot holding it in place. I want to believe that I am growing a root like that into the ground of my being.

The tree tells me that new flowers are new flowers no matter what we look like, and that beauty comes in many forms.

There are other fruit trees here on the lawn. Two pears. One peach. Two plums. They are younger trees and they, too, are in bloom just now.

But the long-lived quince tree is different. It is a *presence* that seems to come forward to meet me. I find myself talking to the tree, addressing it with deference. "Old Grandmother," I say, "how are you this fine Mother's Day?" I swear the tree answers with a little groan, or a sigh. Not a complaint. It is an old tree talking.

"Nice flowers," I say.

"They'll do," mutters the tree. (Matter-of-fact tone that indicates there is no need to gild the lily.)

"Anything you want?" I continue.

"A little water would be nice. Just leave the hose running a few minutes. And don't fuss. That's the main thing. Don't fuss. Things are just fine the way they are. Remember that."

"I'll try to," I say. "But how do I know that they are just fine?"

"You don't until you find it out."

"Please explain, Old Grandmother."

"I will, but only this once. The more you worry the more worry you have. So don't fuss. Just do or don't do. That's all. Second-guessing wastes your life. I'm blooming and that's it. Enough."

"Yes, Grandmother," I say, and fetch the garden hose. But I don't leave it. I stand there and water. Just that. I do this. I water on this fine day in May. Mother's Day.

Turning Soil

*N*ow spring is really here. Everything smells verdant and fresh. I am drawn outside to grub in the ground. It's the green time, the time to turn the soil in the vegetable garden.

Under the leaves of the compost lies new earth. I spade it up bit by bit and heap it up in the wheelbarrow. The soil smells of moisture and nutrients. I am enjoying how black it is . . . full of organic materials . . . full of potential.

Down the little hill I go with the weight of the blue wheelbarrow tugging at my arms. How to design this year's vegetable garden? Two hills for zucchinis, one row for sugar peas, one for beans, one for both

New Zealand spinach and chard to share, one for lettuce. Nooks and crannies for cucumbers, which can climb up and over the protective stone wall.

I spread the new earth on last year's rows. Grubbing in the ground. It feels wonderful. I've become a kid with permission to be dirty. I am getting more than exercise here. Earth-connected, soil-sprinkled, humus-spread, I am turning everything over.

The rows look handsome now, mounded up and ready. I feel hopeful. Expectant. It's preparation time when all is possible. Next to the trowel lies an assortment of seed packets and small flats of tomatoes, basil, and eggplants. The seeds are all different. Beans, sturdy and singular. They can be planted one at a time with precision. I can place each white, kidney-shaped seed. The lettuce seeds, on the other hand, are almost poured into place from the packet. A fine dark dusting is sprinkled down the row to be covered loosely with earth.

Depth of planting, time of planting, proximity of plants to one another. These are all considerations. Eggplants must be moved every year. Tomatoes like the same old place in the garden and flourish well with basil as the companion plant. Snow peas and lettuce like the cool of early summer. New Zealand spinach prefers the later, warmer part. Zucchini does well in slightly sandy soil as do the root crops. It's hard to keep track of all these preferences. But they make the difference between a fine yield and a mediocre one.

Each one of these seed varieties has its own nature, its own way in the garden. If I want a good crop I have to learn about this. My inner nature, too, has its organic leanings. To go against my self will harm my development. I must acknowledge this in me and in others. To really yield we must respect our own nature.

I poke holes to drop the seeds in. Covered by new soil, each in their own place, the seeds wait for sun, for rain, and for their life force to produce the first delicate showing of green. I love this mystery. Each day I will come here to witness it.

It's grubbing-in-the-ground time. Thoroughly dirty from it all, I sprinkle a little earth on myself for good measure. Why not? I am planted in this garden too.

Impatiens

*A*ll danger of frost over, the time has come to plant the impatiens. The property is very shady, and these annuals fill in and give color to the place. They like the conditions and do very well here.

I get many flats of them. For the most part they are the pink, salmon-colored variety. Occasionally I buy white ones as well. Into the tubs and beds they go. It is rather simple-minded ... an all-of-a-kind gardening.

For years I tried other things. I wanted variety and flamboyant color. Of course, the most riotous bloomers are plants that need sun. Since my yard is full of shade nothing much came of those experiments.

I had to submit to planting the one annual that does splendidly here—the humble impatiens.

I can feel my exasperation at being about to do the very same kind of flower planting again this year. My need for variety is thwarted by very real conditions. Impatiens plants need shade and they luxuriate here. With their small, four-petaled flowers they make the place beautiful. And their very profusion creates a special richness. Why do I resist the obvious? I plant the flats and try for some equanimity . . . while knowing there's an irony here . . . I am impatient with these impatiens.

This feeling is familiar. I have it every now and then when I meditate. Something within me resists repeating the same old thing—following the breath, keeping the mind focused, sitting still. I resist the repetition because in the very act of repetition I discover over and over again what the real conditions are within me . . . restlessness . . . need for reassurance . . . fear that life is passing me by and that I am missing something . . . the need for distraction, for entertainment. My mind tries to find ways around itself, resisting the truth. All the shaded parts of my awareness come to light as I sit still, as I repeat the practice over and over again.

The circumstances of this garden suit impatiens to a T. The circumstances of my life could suit me to a T, too, if I would allow myself just to be here. I could enjoy this one-of-a-kind gardening and feel its rightness.

I could simply enjoy living alone instead of questioning it, wondering if I am doing something wrong. I could find relaxation in conducting my work as a therapist . . . letting the hours of faithful attendance to others accumulate in meaning both for me and for them. Life could be simple, without effort. Easy. Why don't I garden and live in this direct way: take up the very same thing again and again and again, and slowly come through to the heart where all things flourish?

I don't have any answers. Resistance is so familiar. It keeps me from feeling the fear of surrendering to the obvious, the fluid way: just doing what needs doing, lending myself year after year to what can grow within me and around me. That means planting impatiens just now. But this acceptance of ease is frightening to me, for behind its apparent appeal lies a light-filled void. There a personality could truly disappear. Nothing to do. Nowhere to go. No one to be . . . the death of *me*. The beginning of spring.

Peonies

With a bundle of stakes under my arm and a green ball of twine in hand I go to the peony bed. It lies in full sun and is shaped like a crescent moon. I stand there and see how leggy the peonies have gotten. Their buds are hard and heavy. Already the plants are bending toward the ground. They need support and it is time to stake them.

For weeks I have been watching the peonies emerge. At first they are just a hint of red in the dark soil. Then more happens. Something round and head-like pushes upward into the world. It looks bloody. Like a birth. Not just one, but many, many births.

Not long after, solid red stems stand erect in the

moon-shaped bed. Their shapes are visible through the living room window even in the dark. I always think of them as a tribe of red people who have ascended from below—materialized their spirits to this place—tunneled up from some dream state or territory that has once given them life. Then they are here, eager to live in the new world.

We are born this way, too, emerging into this life from some other place, ready to live where we are planted. Ready to be at risk and think nothing of it. At least to begin with.

Now it is June. The solstice will soon be here. The peony leaves are growing dark green and glossy. There are fewer leaves on the plants this year and this gives the illusion that the plants are taller. I hide a stake in the middle of a peony clump, cut the twine, and gather the plants in my arms. A peony hug! The fingers of my two hands try to find each other while my face is deep in the leaves. I feel my way to making a knot. The circle of twine must close but not too tightly. A little tug to make sure that it will hold, and I let the plants go. They spring back and right them-selves. They look braced, and I am aware that I have been embraced by peony leaves along my whole torso. A fair exchange.

"Peony hugging," I think to myself as I move from clump to clump. Each place I become more aware of the hard and heavy buds. Their weight has already begun to bend the stems toward the ground. In a few days the blossoms will open, and they will be huge. The whole plant will groan.

I think of human blossoming and how much it, too, needs to be staked and supported. We need a circle of friends to hold us if we are going to open like peony buds and let out the beauty that is in us.

How many of us have keeled over just in the time of blooming for lack of support and encouragement? How many of us have not dared to reveal our true selves because we fear being cut, we fear the dying afterward? How many of us say to life, "This is a mistake. I can't do it. It takes more than I've got"?

It does take everything we've got. I walk around the bed. It is a cradle. The plants reach my navel now. Some have only one bud. Some have two, and some have as many as six blossoms. Their peony natures have said "yes" and have opened. The petals radiate out—white with pink—pink with white. I want to find the nature in me that will say "yes" like this. And I want to support others in their blooming . . . to be a stake, a circle of twine, an encouragement, a witness.

SUMMER

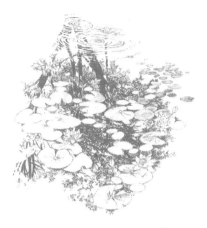

The Pond

A path leads through the underbrush, under the tall canopy of the mastlike ash trees. Summer has come. July, but I am no longer sure if it is this year, last year, or next year. It does not matter. The little pond is dark, a muddy color. I can see the leaves of many autumns in the bottom of it, russet, brown and gray. On its surface are water lilies. They float like dreams, lit by a yellow white light. From time to time a bubble rises from the murky bottom as if the roots wanted to share in the light too.

Much is always happening here. The spring peepers are not as noticeable now—the heavy plop at the far shore tells me the bullfrogs have reached maturity. From time to time a "glunk" rises like the sound of deep swallowing. And then the chorus starts—like sawing near the waterline.

A young maple leans out over the pond to create a leafy umbrella. Its shadow makes the water's surface reflect more purely. Sky and trees are drawn down here to the level of my feet, yet they are also above me. A dragonfly—electric blue with black wings—lands on a witch hazel leaf next to my thigh. An ancient insect, its color is startling—a shock of iridescent brightness in the shade upon shade of apple green, hunter green, blue green under yet deeper purple green and black green. Layer upon layer of color. For a moment I recall my mother's palette, her buildup of paint so that light could shine through. I see that light here in this place. Green folding in upon green.

Below the dreamy, lily-padded water lives a large snapping turtle. I have seen it cruising the bottom like a darkness within a darkness. It is somehow satisfying to think of its beak, its clawed feet moving indolently forward, the eyes and carapace almost unchanged in its species for millennia. I am afraid of and yet savor this wildness. The time of ancient beasts is still here in this suburban backyard. Dragonfly and snapping turtle. I feel stirred when I sense these connections and I feel hopeful too. Perhaps I haven't been tamed yet either.

I have time for reverie here, for gazing on the

world in a new way. I dream into the pond as into an eye. Minutes expand into hours, into time that is not measured. The dark water opens as if something were gazing back at me. I feel I am looking into the ground's eye, the eye of a huge presence. I am suddenly shy and very small. Exposed, stripped, not of my clothes, but of something else—of a layer that separates me from the world. I shiver and grow quiet. I feel naked and penetratingly seen.

To gaze into the eye of the ground itself, is it possible? Can the ground be aware of me? This is too strange to speak about. But I do sense the mutuality. This presence upholds my creatureliness . . . it knows that I breathe and move . . . that I cry and love . . . that I am afraid and exultant . . . that I create and destroy . . . that I hurt and take care. It knows! But not in any way that I can explain.

I feel an urgency now. I am compelled to notice everything. The wellspring that feeds the pond, and the land that holds this water. I am drawn into the sedge grass, the stones, the moss, and the tree roots that describe the edge of this place. I absorb the brown leaves that make the water dark and reflective. I am imprinted with the maple's shadow, plopped by frogs, sheltered by sky, and delighted by dragonflies. I am taken to the depth that mirrors my face back to me. And I sense the "snapper" moving like a mysterious cloud in the water.

This is happening inside me. The living water rises in my blood, the dragonfly whirs in my inner ear, the high-pitched joy of the peeper trills in my cells, the leaves mat and settle in my belly. I can feel how my life is a shared event. I am separate from nothing, not even the dead. Pondlike, reflective, who is this me? I don't know. I don't know. . . .

Noon. The heat seems to glaze the surface of the water. In the quiet and dark heart of the pond, Saint Snapper settles down. I wonder if deep inside me I am settling, too, learning to be fluid and yet still?

Day Lilies

*H*eight of summer. The day lilies are budding. They will soon come out. There are three varieties that will stagger their blooming from now until the beginning of August. All three are yellow: bright yellow. Butter yellow. And salmon yellow. They are a celebration of the sun at its zenith, their brief life an acknowledgment that each day is a unique blossom.

There is a ring of them near the crescent bed of peonies. There is a bank of them along one stone wall. And since they are profuse and readily multiply I have moved some to the bare place near the brook. I could have day lilies everywhere there is sun, just as I have impatiens everywhere there is shade.

Their stalks are thick and woody. Each one has several buds . . . the size of ladyfingers. One can eat these flowers. They have a mild, delicious flavor, as if one were tasting the sun. Their tubers can be dug up, and the small rhizomes they produce are also edible. They are nutty and white when young . . . like new potatoes.

Middle of summer is yellow-glory time. These lilies are bountiful. When I bring one in and put it in a vase, it illuminates my table, as though the sun were shining inside my house. Saint Glow. The lily will stay large and open until midnight. By morning, however, it is limp and wizened, and leaves a clear, round drop of moisture on the table. My finger touches it and I remember touching the corpse of my mother—the mystery of life passed on. I do not take these flowers for granted. It is all here together—my mother, this lily, and this day.

The solstice has passed. Now the year turns again toward the dark. More than ever I treasure these days as they grow shorter. In my own life I know I have fewer days left now than I have lived.

I look inside the yellowest of the lilies. It is trumpet-shaped. Looking deep I see the stamen, the pistil, and I see the mysterious darkness in the neck of the trumpet. Is it from there that all this yellow light pours out?

Black Snake

*H*e lives in the stone wall. A very large snake. In the heat of late July he can sometimes be found baking on the stones. He has a drugged, sleepy quality when I find him in this state. He is letting his cold-blooded nature absorb the delicious warmth of these high summer days.

Black snake and I are friends. He does not bother me and I do not bother him, but we are aware of each other. He no longer slithers away when I find him. In this mutual living arrangement we admire each other, and keep the appropriate distance.

Other snakes have always frightened me, but this one does not. He seems a guardian. Every house should have its own black snake. I know he keeps the mice and chipmunk population down. But he does more. To me he is a representative of ancient wisdom. His very being reminds me that renewal is possible, that skins can and ought to be shed. I once found one of his . . . transparent . . . paper thin.

Black snake is elegant, whether coiled or moving. Like a small dark river he pours himself into the stone wall when he wants to, and is gone. The movement is sensuous. He flows himself forward, his belly feels and knows every inch of the ground. This is intimate indeed.

Sometimes I lie down on the grass to feel the ground with my own belly—in a kind of serpent connection. Skin on skin: earth skin, human skin.

To be held by earth, to shed your old skins and wait for the sun, to be cold when it is cold, to move quickly when it is time to move, and to lie about in happy indolence, this is black snake knowledge.

We meet at the stone wall . . . the warm-blooded one and the cold-blooded one . . . our domains joined for a moment. What do we have in common? The stones and the sun's warmth. The July air and the high cumulus clouds. We have this moment to be friends, to please each other. Black snake, I want you to know you please me very greatly.

Yellow Jackets

There is now no picnic without at least three yellow jackets. It is the high heat of summer, the end of July. These insects hover around the food. They land in the fruit salad. They wedge themselves between the hamburger buns. Seemingly they will not be stopped.

These wasps have their nests in the ground. I have seen them fly into a very small hole in the bank under the wild roses. There is another nest under the pear tree. There may even be a third. Their nests are true "safe houses," and are strategically placed. The wasps can absorb their food and fly straight home.

It is curious to me that these insects like sugar

and meat in equal measure. Whatever they can take, they take. They are pesky pests. Saint Sting! I do not like the yellow jacket. I struggle with its species. I have poured gasoline into their homes and struck a match. My son, in an effort to help with this problem, was stung very terribly. Saint Yellow Jacket, I am stuck with your kind and I do not like you.

These wasps share my yard, my food, and my leisure . . . turning pleasant repasts into mobilizations for self-defense. Saint Sting affords me the opportunity to practice endurance and persistence.

Of course, I could forgo eating outside. But that gives these winged terrors too much power. And besides it is now very hot inside. What is it then that I endure? I do not believe it is Saint Sting actually. I have to endure my own discomfort and my fear of being stung, which fear is not unrealistic.

I have to endure interference with my personal rhythm. When I raise my fork to my mouth and a wasp goes with the eating utensil, I have to put it down. I have to wait. My eating pattern, and other patterns as well, are rattled.

I have to endure my guests' discomfort also. I find myself embarrassed that I have *wasps,* as if they were some communicable disease.

I have to endure the creepy feeling that my air space is being violated. One has a kinesthetic sense of how much space around the body is one's own . . . not unlike the air space and water rights of cities. These wasps are in my aura and I cannot keep them out.

In all this I can watch their persistence. They are not daunted by rolled newspapers, fly swatters, lemon-scented candles intended to discourage little flying things. They know where they are going. FOR THE STUFF!!!!!!!!!!!!!!

If I could ever apply myself with similar concentration I would frighten myself. They have a kind of white heat about them. Their intensity matches the thermometer reading. Ninety degrees Fahrenheit and climbing. One hundred degrees of heat and concentration. I must take my sun hat off to these creatures of God's making. I acknowledge their right to be in this world, but I do not have to like them. Go away. Sting!

Vines

—————————

*H*oneysuckle and wild grape grow here in profusion. In and of themselves they are wonderful vines. The night air fills with honeysuckle sweetness, and by day bees visit them from my neighbor's hive. In August the grapes produce heavy purple clusters for jelly and the large, edible leaves for dolmades.

And yet the trees and bushes are choked by these vines. I am constantly having to cut them back. Whack! Whack! There is a persistent clinging going on here, to the point where some trees and bushes perish under the weight. I can feel how silently the vines take over if I am not on my guard.

When I go to prune them back I see how skillfully they wrap themselves clockwise around whatever is available. They are the opportunists of the garden, the hangers-on. Tendrils reach out to secure more growing territory. Up the trunk, over the branch, out into the air, searching for any cling-on place. No respecters of boundaries, these. They are the great enmeshers, thoughtless, relentless, helical, and wondrous.

I have to whack, and I do it with abandon. No nice careful pruning here. This is a machete kind of boundary setting that needs to be done on a regular basis. The pile of cut vines can grow to bonfire size. No reason to feel any compunction. They will be back. Whack!

I am struck by how hard it is for me to be similarly relentless when it comes to clinging people. There are always one or two with whom I struggle over boundaries. They are the honeysuckle and the grape in my personal relationships. I want them to be part of my life but I do not want them to weigh me to the ground.

I say no, politely, to begin with. I set up barriers. I raise my voice. Often the boundary is not respected, even then. So I go out into my garden to study the vines. I see and verify that the nature of honeysuckle and grape is to climb, to grow *upon* something. They cannot be other than how they are. Therefore they must be contained in a proper way. I do not need to get angry about this. I just have to do the job. But I am not a whacker by nature. So this is hard.

When I think about it, we are all actually vine-like. We grow upon the strength of others, reaching out for new places of discovery. Our need for support is constant. I want to remember that there is no skipping the boundary setting, even with nearest and dearest. This is "tough love" for me.

But when I study the vines in my garden I see that they actually become stronger the more I contain them. Rather than spreading farther out, the vines gain substance. They get thicker and sturdier. They hold themselves up a little better. I want to trust what I see. I want to trust that this also happens when I refuse to let people take advantage of me, disregard me, or assume that I am continually available for support.

Whack! I shiver at the pruning task. It is so deliberate, so steely, so necessary. I hurt for myself and for the other. Whack! The feeling of being weighed down goes. Whack! Enmeshments go. Whack! Hard as it is, we grow stronger for the pruning.

And the summer nights continue warm and full of stars. I smell the honeysuckle through my window. I am glad. And in the morning I go hunting for the young grapes. They are filling out, plump and dusty purple.

Cicadas

*N*ow in the cycle of seasons since my mother's death the anniversary of her birthday comes. August fifth. I light a candle for her and feel bereft. I miss her greatly, miss her laugh, her big warm hands, her lust for life. I miss her shape in a doorway. I miss the way she walked, tiptoeing lightly like a girl, even in her portly seventies. To know she is no longer is strange. It makes the world itself strange.

The heat has been relentless. Everything seems to pant or wilt or move with appalling effort. At night the cicadas have started their chorus. It is a rather quiet chorus to begin with, but as summer progresses toward autumn the singing seems to intensify, till nights are filled to capacity by the chorus. Each night is a chamber of sound—waves move into each other and also echo one another. Sound arises and falls away, only to return again. How many cicadas are out there? How many?

I feel sad now. Burdened, actually. The heat has something to do with it. I do not want to move my body and yet I must bear up. It's too hot to work, to play, to plant, to do anything at all. I feel as if I am both in the bed and by the bed of someone dying. A truly helpless feeling.

August is often when wars start, when old folks die, when there are violent storms. Everything seems to have difficulty enduring itself. Ripeness is a burdensome state. It has too much potential violence in it.

Many people go away on vacation now. I feel I cannot do anything about anything. I might as well lie in the hammock and listen to cicadas singing out their monotony, their exultation. This is their time . . . the chanting time.

I think of ceremonies I have attended where the drum held a beat for hours, and the same song was sung until one gave into it, until the inner door swung wide and another dimension opened up. Scientific theories tell how a critical mass must be arrived at before a new paradigm can be discovered. If this is true for science, for creativity, and for consciousness, it must be true for the state of grief also. I live each day and feel the hum of life around me, and I feel my mother's absence just as keenly.

One bears grief in whatever way one can, as long as one must. Silently it accumulates. If it has no direct means of expression it will come out in an illness, in an accident, in the rupture of a relationship. Grief ripens like a fruit. It must be harvested in some way. We need company to do this, for to grieve alone only drives the pain into a deeper place.

The cicadas are wailing. This is my time to feel the weight of grief. This season I need a friend to be with, someone who will not be shocked if I keen too. I want to wail in waves like the cicadas, and let the grief out so I can hear it . . . the grief of such loss, the grief of all that suffers . . . the salutary grief that when acknowledged gives relief, an opening to life.

Honeybells

*A*long the stone wall grow the hosta. They have been filling out more and more as the years go by. Big leaves emerge in May and get larger, until by June a deep bank of green lines the wall. Some of the leaves have dark edges, some are as big as elephant ears.

These plants give shape to the garden. They are large, handsome, and sturdy. Their flowers smell sweet. On moonlit nights, late like this in the summer, you can see the whitish purple bells shine back. They deserve the name the nursery gave them, honeybell.

When they have gone by, the flowers produce

seeds that birds like. All in all these are steady, no-fuss, no-work plants that make the garden look shapely and complete no matter what may or may not be blooming.

As a consequence these hosta are easy to take for granted. Anything strong, steady, reliable, constant, is taken for granted. There is an of-course-you'll-continue-to-be-there attitude one develops with such dependability.

There are people who are like these plants. We do not even know how much we count on them. They are the background, the backbone, the backup. And they become somehow invisible to us in their strength and willingness to serve. We are totally surprised if anything happens to them. We are shocked, in fact.

One year some deer came in July and munched up the hosta. The leaves had come to maturity, and since all the succulent greens had been exhausted in the woods, the deer came to help themselves to this ready green grocery. I woke up that morning and found what looked like trimmed celery stalks. No large green elephant leaves. No dense green sculpture. Only stalks! The place was devastated.

After that I took more care. I got human hair from the barber to put on the ground. (The smell is said to discourage the deer.) I began to appreciate the stately shapes of these sturdy plants. I began to care more for them than for the annuals. I no longer took their steady presence for granted.

And I have to think now about relationships I have taken for granted. My mother certainly. Old friends. People in the helping professions whom I expect to be reliable: my dentist, my doctor, the person who does my taxes, the man who has cut the grass for years. They form the background to my foreground, and I understand how much I have not realized the shape that they give my life.

Saint Honeybell. The stems of hosta flowers are waving in the August breeze. A sweet aroma wafts over my garden wall. This delicate odor is the silent ringing of these bells. "Wake up," they say. "Hear the bell. Appreciate us. There is yet time."

Harvest

---

*C*ucumbers, tomatoes, basil, eggplant, peppers, beets, New Zealand spinach. The crops are coming in now. I have not done so well with the vegetable garden, but well enough to feel rushed, to want to use the produce, to invite people over to help me eat it.

The nasturtiums are in full bloom. Their snappy leaves and flowers fill the salad bowl. The tomatoes are bulging with juice. The pears are yellowing. The plums have already gone by. There is plenty now. It's bounty time. When the time for bounty is here I must not dread what might come next. This is the time to open wide, to harvest, to share, to be as flagrant as nature. It is early September, the time of ripeness when all hangs ready on the plant. Take it.

As I pick cucumbers, their prickly skins caress my hand. My eggplants hang in purple splendor, not as big this year as other times, but glossy and silky of skin. I remember when they were only mauve four-petaled flowers. I pop a nasturtium in my mouth. "Nasty urchins," as my friend Joyce calls them. The roof of my mouth pings with the stimulation. My basket is full of saints. Each mature vegetable or fruit has touched me first as seedling or seed. As they grew, I grew. We have ripened together.

I gather this harvest to me. I will consume it and make it part of my very flesh even as I harvest experience and it, too, becomes part of my very being. I know I live by consuming life. And life is living me, consuming me.

I hold the bounty basket in my arms. On top are the nasturtium flowers. They move in the breeze that has just come over the hill. The red, yellow, orange flowers roll to the basket's rim. Quickly I put a hand over them so they will not blow to the ground. The breeze picks up. The petals shiver. My basket is full. It is all so precious and impermanent. With my hand over this riot of color, I feel this year—the grief and the joy of it—the great bounty.

FALL AGAIN

Compost

*N*ow I weed out the flower beds, getting ready for the frost. The vegetable garden has been turned over. The impatiens are setting seed pods. In my fist these pods explode like small, green firecrackers. Freed, the little black seeds lie in the crevice of my hand, highlighting the crease the palmists call the lifeline.

Small songbirds help themselves to the honeybell seeds, and squirrels are avidly gathering acorns. I pop the last of the late raspberries into my mouth. They are poignantly sweet. Now the ash tree boletus emerge from the ground, and puffballs. These mushrooms are edible, and I harvest them, too.

It's cleanup time. I trudge with my wheelbarrow up to the compost pile—a handsome heap by now. Leaves have begun to fall. I bring vegetable scraps and garden remains to this, my kitchen midden. The leaves from last year are now flattened on the ground, somewhat decomposed, and underneath all is a haven for earthworms. I turn the compost with the pitchfork. I see the black earth and the slow undulating movement of the worms. They are long and fat at this time of year. Science tells us that by mass there are more worms than any other living thing.

I lift the top layer of leaves with the pitchfork. The work of decomposition has been going on quietly all these months—a silent heat. It has broken down all the old organic material and there is new earth here. I will put this soil on the garden come spring. But now I bring my prunings, gleanings, and kitchen scraps, and pile them up. Soon leaves will cover everything and the slow transformation will continue, the composting of another year.

Twelve months have passed. I have lived all the seasons. Standing here in this kitchen midden, knee-high in leaves, I know this year now joins all the other years. It's fall again. The geese fly over, heading south. Their honking lifts my spirits. I think of my mother and somehow I feel her presence inside me. I know now that everything that was is still present in some fundamental and mysterious way.

This is intimacy: its touch is ever new, reveal-ing the precious moments we have to live and to connect with all things. No love is ever lost in this universe. No matter what season, what year, what place, love will always be turned into new soil. Grate-ful to the saints of this place, and feeling intimacy grow with all that lives and has lived here, I hold my mother closely in my heart and mind, and I sense the passion, the silent becoming in this compost, in the living of the years.

About the Author

Gunilla Norris is a psychotherapist in private practice. She now lives in Mystic, Connecticut, where she works as a writer. This is the fourth book in her series of meditations on living every day in awareness of the divine. It follows publication of *Being Home, Becoming Bread,* and *Sharing Silence.* She has also written eleven children's books and one book of poems, *Learning from the Angel.*

OTHER BELL TOWER BOOKS

Books that nourish the soul, illuminate the mind,
and speak directly to the heart

Valeria Alfeyeva. **Pilgrimage to Dzhvari:** *A Woman's Journey of Spiritual Awakening.* Hardcover 0-517-59194-4 (1993).

David A. Cooper. **Silence, Simplicity, and Solitude:** *A Guide for Spiritual Retreat.* Hardcover 0-517-58620-7 (1992); paperback 0-517-88186-1 (1994).

The Heart of Stillness: *The Elements of Spiritual Practice.* Hardcover 0-517-58621-5 (1992); paperback 0-517-88187-X (1994).

Entering the Sacred Mountain: *A Mystical Odyssey.* Hardcover 0-517-59653-9 (1994).

James G. Cowan. **Letters From a Wild State:** *Rediscovering Our True Relationship to Nature.* Hardcover 0-517-58770-X (1992).

Messengers of the Gods: *Tribal Elders Reveal the Ancient Wisdom of the Earth.* Softcover 0-517-88078-4 (1993).

Marc David. **Nourishing Wisdom:** *A Mind/Body Approach to Nutrition and Well-Being.* Hardcover 0-517-57636-8 (1991); softcover 0-517-88129-2 (1994).

Kat Duff. **The Alchemy of Illness**. Softcover 0-517-88097-0 (1993).

Noela N. Evans. **Meditations for the Passages and Celebrations of Life:** *A Book of Vigils.* Hardcover 0-517-59341-6 (1994).

Burghild Nina Holzer. **A Walk Between Heaven and Earth:** *A Personal Journal on Writing and the Creative Process.* Softcover 0-517-88096-2 (1994).

Greg Johanson and Ron Kurtz. **Grace Unfolding:** *Psychotherapy in the Spirit of the Tao-te ching.* Hardcover 0-517-58449-2 (1991); softcover 0-517-88130-6 (1994).

Marcia and Jack Kelly. **Sanctuaries—The Northeast:** *A Guide to Lodgings in Monasteries, Abbeys, and Retreats of the United States.* Softcover 0-517-57727-5 (1991).

Sanctuaries—The West Coast and Southwest. Softcover 0-517-88007-5 (1993).

One Hundred Graces, eds., with calligraphy by Christopher Gausby. Hardcover 0-517-58567-7 (1992).

Barbara Lachman. **The Journal of Hildegard of Bingen.** Hardcover 0-517-59169-3 (1993).

Gunilla Norris. **Being Home:** *A Book of Meditations.* Hardcover 0-517-58159-0 (1991).

Becoming Bread: *Meditations on Loving and Transformation.* Hardcover 0-517-59168-5 (1993).

Sharing Silence: *Meditation Practice and Mindful Living.* Hardcover 0-517-59506-0 (1993).

Ram Dass and Mirabai Bush. **Compassion in Action:** *Setting Out on the Path of Service.* Softcover 0-517-57635-X (1992).

Richard Whelan, ed. **Self-Reliance:** *The Wisdom of Ralph Waldo Emerson as Inspiration for Daily Living.* Softcover 0-517-58512-X (1991).